Pete and Tootsie

by

Blaine and Sarah Tucker

Illustrated by Emily Gruver

Koinonia Associates, LLC
Knoxville, Tennessee

ISBN 978-1-60658-022-6

Published by:
Koinonia Associates
7809 Timber Glow Trail
Knoxville, TN 37938

To learn how you can become a published
author, visit PublishwithKA.com
October 31, 2011

Illustrated by Emily Gruver

Dedication

This book is dedicated in loving memory of Mom and Dad, who worked to make a loving home for us eight kids, and hemmed us all in with much prayer.

Acknowledgments

First of all, we express thanks to God who has given us life and the experiences upon which this book is based. He deserves all the glory!

Many thanks to our grandchildren Charissa (age 9), Ben (age 10), and David (age 15), who provided valuable editorial assistance as did our Nanette. This book was made far richer because of your input. Thanks to Christana for technical assistance and to Jonathan for formatting. Thanks to our daughter's Jack Russell terrier Emma who became the stand-in for the starring role of Tootsie. There were so many similarities between the two dogs. Thanks also to Wendy for the photography. Thanks to Ann and Nathan for traipsing over the Kentucky hills with us, locating photo sites and the old homeplace in order to give authenticity to the original setting for the story. Thanks to Brent for creating our web page and for encouraging us on the road to publication.

Much appreciation goes to all family and friends who contributed in any way to this our maiden voyage into writing; you know who you are. This book would not be in reader's hands without your support, encouragement, and prayers.

Table of Contents

Chapter One

A Tiny Surprise Comes Home

The year was 1947 and Harry Truman was president of the United States. The 40 years of Cold War began with Russia and Jackie Robinson took the field for the Brooklyn Dodgers becoming the first Negro to play Major League Baseball. There were forest fires in Maine, hurricanes in Florida, and really bad snowstorms in the northeastern part of the country. A loaf of bread cost thirteen cents, a postage stamp was three and a gallon of gas cost just fifteen. Things were changing but none of that was important to 12-year old Pete...at least not right now!

Pete lived on a farm right at the edge of the

Daniel Boone Forest. That made for good, wide open spaces where a boy could roam! Pete's family lived in a snug house that his Dad built. Mom stayed home and took care of baby brother Wayne while Pete, Jim, Martha, and Meg went to school on a big yellow school bus. They had food to eat, clothes to wear, and lots of love to make them happy. Life was good there in his part of Kentucky.

When Pete came home from school each day, his faithful dog Tootsie was waiting for him. Somewhere, as he walked along the road to the house, Tootsie would appear. Tootsie was the only dog Pete had ever had. She was a small, white, short-haired terrier-type dog that stood about 10 inches high and was 18 inches long. Pete never knew if Tootsie was a special breed of dog but that didn't really matter to him. They had many playful days and adventures that made life happy for Pete and some days, Tootsie seemed like the most important thing in Pete's world. He just loved her so much!

Pete could remember the day that Tootsie became his dog just as clearly as if it were yesterday. It happened about a year ago now. Dad had a job as a coal miner, and every day he went to dig coal from the underground mines. Then it was sold by the Coal Mining Company for people to use in their homes for heat. One day, when he came home from work, he called out, "Hey, Pete, come out here in the yard a minute. I have something really special to show you!"

Pete hurried outside to where Dad stood.

Dad said, "Pete reach into my jacket pocket and you will find a surprise."

"What is it, Dad?" asked Pete before he even looked in Dad's pocket.

"It is something I think you're going to like very much. Come on now, it won't bite or anything," said Dad.

Pete could see Dad's jacket moving and when he put his hand into the pocket, he pulled out a little, white, ball of fur. He was getting excited as he thought of what it might be. Taking a good look at the wiggly mass of fur, Pete realized he was holding a very tiny, white puppy with a black nose.

"Oh, would you just look at this! It's a little puppy. It's really cute! Did you bring it for me, Dad?" Pete asked.

"Yes," Dad replied. "A fellow brought her into work today and I knew when I saw her that she might grow to be a fine dog for you. Well, what do you think?"

"I think yes," said Pete with much joy in his voice. "Did you just say that this is a girl puppy?"

"Yes, the fellow who gave her to me said there was a family of five puppies and they needed to find them good homes. She is about six weeks old and will always be a little, short-haired dog. I thought you might like to have a pet of your own. Now that you have been doing the milking on time, you have become so responsible with all your chores that I thought you deserved a reward," Dad answered.

"You bet I would love my own dog," said Pete. "I will take really good care of her and give her water and food every day. What can she eat, Dad?"

"Since she no longer needs to nurse from her mother, I believe she can have the scraps of food from our supper table. You'll need to be careful that you don't let her have little bones that could get stuck in her throat, and she will need something to gnaw on to help her teeth grow strong. Other than that and a lot of love and attention, I don't think she will need anything else," said Dad.

"Wow! My very own dog! I can hardly believe it! She's my very own dog!" Pete shouted over and over as he ran into the house to show the rest of the family.

Everyone in Pete's family came to have a look. They petted her and took turns holding her and telling Pete how wonderful it was that he had a dog. They asked Dad the same kinds of questions Pete had which he patiently answered again. They were glad for Pete. Dad knew the girls didn't want a puppy. After all, they had their cat Willow and that seemed to keep them happy. Brother Jim was two years older than Pete and he would be graduating high school this year and leaving home soon. But now, Pete had a pet of his own too. Oh, yes!

He had his very own dog!

"Does she already have a name, Dad?" asked Pete.

"Well, the guy at work said his kids had named all the puppies and had been calling this one *Tootsie.* But, she's your dog and it won't matter to her. Whatever you want to call her will be the name she will get used to as she grows.

"Hmm," thought Pete, "Tootsie sounds like a different name for a dog but I believe I might like it. I may just keep calling her by that name. We'll get used to it together. Tootsie, yeah, that might be a good name for this little ball of fur. I believe I like it already."

Pete carried Tootsie back outside and sat down on the porch with her. He petted her and talked and talked to her then carried her with him while he went to find a pan for her water and something to help make a place on the porch where she could sleep. He began to day-dream about all the things a boy would do with a pet dog.

"Well," Pete told Tootsie, "you are not going to be big enough to be a real hunting dog so we will just have to see what other adventures we can have together." That was what was on Pete's mind that night as he tried hard to settle down and get to sleep. Life was going to be even better now that he had a pet of his very own.

Chapter Two

Bonding

The next few weeks had flown by as Pete and Tootsie became acquainted with one another. He loved the feel of her soft white fur and warm wiggly body. It tickled his nose every time she gave kisses on his face with that little, dry tongue of hers. From the start, she acted like she knew she was his. Her little brown eyes followed his every move and she was quick to try and toddle along after him wherever he went.

At first, she was so tiny that Pete was afraid to leave her outside, even on the porch. He thought she might squeeze through the railings and get hurt if she dropped off. One end of the porch was about four feet off the ground but the yard slanted so much that at the other end, there was a drop of about seven feet. That was enough to really cause Tootsie harm if she fell.

"Mom, do you think I could sleep with Tootsie in my bed while she is little so I can watch over her through the night?" Pete asked.

"What do you think might happen if you rolled over on her?" asked his Mom. "You are much bigger than she is, and you know that you sleep so soundly that you rarely hear noises in the night. If she got tucked into one of the hollows made by your feather bed, you wouldn't even know you were crushing her."

Pete's bed had a box springs but the mattress was a feather bed. That meant it was like a gigantic bed-sized pillow stuffed with duck or goose feathers. Pete liked it because he could snuggle down deeply into it and get warm. He thought about what Mom said for a few minutes then answered, "You're right! I hadn't thought about that, and it sure would make me sad if I crushed her. Well, then what about if I put a box on the floor right beside my bed?" he wondered aloud.

"Try that tonight and see if it works out okay If Tootsie likes it there, you can keep her in the house until she gets big enough to stay outside," replied Mom.

That made Pete really happy, so he went outside to look all around the farm for something he could use for Tootsie's bed. In the barn, he found just the thing. His sister Ora had come home from Indiana for a visit a few weeks ago and brought with her a wooden crate of Pepsi bottles; the whole family had enjoyed the unexpected treat. But now, the crate was just lying around, discarded and being used by no one. It would be just the right size for a bed for Tootsie! It would keep her safe while she was little, but would also be big enough for the time when Pete had to move her outside to the porch. Yes, it would do just fine.

He stood there looking around the barn for a few minutes then spotted some empty feed sacks. Dad sometimes had to buy extra feed for the animals; some came in cloth sacks and some in burlap sacks. Pete knew he couldn't use the cloth sacks because Mom used those to make dresses for the girls. He would just have to use an empty burlap sack; that would make the bed soft enough for his little dog. He hurried back to the house with his treasures and soon had everything ready for night time.

At bedtime, Pete nestled Tootsie down into her new bed and then crawled into his own feather bed right beside her. Everything was so new to her that he hoped she would feel good and be able to stay in her bed through the night. But, sometime during the night, Pete was awakened by Tootsie's whimpering. She just wouldn't stop crying. At first, he didn't know what could be wrong with her. She still had plenty of water in her bowl so he knew she wasn't thirsty. He thought she might be missing her Mom or be sick. When he picked her up to check closer, Tootsie was so excited that she wet on his pajamas!

"So, that's what was wrong!" he muttered. "Guess I will learn to take you out before putting you to bed, won't I?"

Pete changed out of his wet clothes, put Tootsie back into her bed then settled himself down again for the rest of the night. It didn't take long for Pete to get into the habit of taking Tootsie out at night, and she soon became his alarm clock by whimpering to be taken out in the mornings. Before bedtime, she was so funny. Tootsie would get sleepy before it was Pete's bedtime but she wasn't about to go to sleep without him! So she sat there with droopy eyes, trying to stay awake until Pete said, "Come on, Tootsie. It's time for us to get to bed." Those were the magic words she had been waiting for, so she toddled right along after him and before long was able to climb into her bed by herself.

Pretty soon Pete and Tootsie settled into a good routine. Everywhere you saw one of them, the other was sure to be close by. Tootsie was a very energetic little dog, and was always alert to every sound and movement around her. When Pete took her outside, she loved to chase. Even from the beginning, she would try to catch anything that moved, like grasshoppers and butterflies. Pete had a feeling that when she got a little bigger, she would be chasing rabbits and most likely even try to catch the few squirrels that came around now and then. She even tried to chase Willow, the family cat, but Willow didn't care for Tootsie's antics. She treated her much like she did one of her kittens, and preferred it when Tootsie would just leave her alone. In time, they learned to live in peace with one another.

One morning, when Pete was getting dressed, he couldn't find one of his socks. Was he surprised when he finally spied it in Tootsie's box! He couldn't figure how it had gotten in there but when he tried to take it from Tootsie, she held on tight. That started a tug-of-war.

"Come on, Tootsie girl," he pleaded. "I need that sock to wear today. Give it up, now. Be careful or you'll tear a hole in it, and I really need that sock."

Gently and carefully Pete managed to remove the sock from Tootsie's teeth without tearing it. But this gave him an idea. He quickly realized that this was a game they could play together so he began to look for something they could use. He found Mom's bag of rags and in it was a pair of old socks that were too worn out to repair anymore. He brought them to Tootsie's bed. After that, he was careful to put his own socks down deeply into his shoes and put the shoes out of her reach so she couldn't get to them again. It was fun to tease Tootsie with the socks. He would pull on one end while she held the other end in her mouth and they had a little tug-of-war. He liked to listen to her growls and watch her stubby little tail wiggle back and forth. When he took her outside, he

learned that she would play the same game with a stick. This was the first of many games they would learn to play together.

"Mom, when are you going to the grocery again?" asked Pete one morning.

"Actually, I need to go to town today, and

was planning to stop in at New's Grocery on the way home. Why do you ask?" she replied.

"Well, I've been thinking that Tootsie needs some big bones to chew on," answered Pete. "Would you mind asking Mr. New if he has some he could give you? Those would be big enough so they won't get stuck in her throat and will help sharpen her teeth."

"I will add that to my list," said Mom. "That's a good idea, especially after what happened at supper the other night."

Pete dropped his head low, rather embarrassed at the reminder of the awful thing Tootsie did at the table. The family had been almost ready to sit down for the evening meal when somehow Tootsie had managed to jump up onto benches and chairs to get over onto the table where food was waiting. Before anyone was aware of what was happening, she went to the platter of chicken, snatched one of the pieces, and then proceeded with leaps and bounds to jump down and run from the room into what she thought would be a safe hiding place where she could enjoy her feast. All this time, Pete had thought she was safely out of the way, in her bed in his room, but she had surprised all of them. Pete thought later that she must have smelled the good food and wanted some of whatever they were having for supper.

Thankfully, there were still enough pieces of chicken left to go around for everyone, but no one thought it was one bit funny . . . at the time. They would later recall the event and laugh about it, but that night, no one was laughing. Dad had a few choice words of caution for Pete along with the suggestion that it was well past time that Tootsie was moved outside for good. There would be no more staying inside for Tootsie.

And so it was that Pete moved Tootsie's bed out onto the porch, where she lived for the rest of her life. He spent some time getting her used to the new location; being sure she had her food and water bowls and was comfortable. He knew he had to teach her to go up and down steps, but until he felt sure she had learned that lesson well, he placed a board at the top of the steps so she wouldn't fall down to the ground. Those high drop offs at either end of the porch would injure her for sure.

By the time Tootsie was about three or four months old, she began developing some brown spots on her body. They were mostly all along the top of her back and around her eyes and ears. Pete thought she was the most beautiful dog ever!

She had finally learned how to go up and down steps so she would follow Pete everywhere he went. She went with him to do his chores but when it was time to mow, Pete had to fasten her on the porch so she wouldn't get herself tangled in the lawnmower. The first time he mowed the yard with her around, he found her shaking all over from the strange noise that she couldn't seem to understand.

One day, Pete tried teaching a new game to Tootsie. He wanted to see if she would fetch something he threw. He took one of the small rubber balls from the toy chest and threw it across the yard while Tootsie stood nearby.

"Go get the ball, girl," Pete called. "Get the ball and bring it back to me. Go on now. Get the ball."

Pete didn't have to wait long before Tootsie started bounding across the grass. He could see where the ball landed and watched as Tootsie quickly found it and scooped it up into her mouth.

"Bring it back here to me," Pete encouraged.

He got down on his knees and begged Tootsie to come to him. She began inching her way to him, crouched down on all four legs while holding fast to the ball. When she got near him, Pete tried to take the ball from her.

"Come on now, give it back to me and I'll throw it again for you. We'll have a new game that you will love," Pete pleaded, "this isn't our tug-of-war game."

Finally he wrestled the ball from her mouth and threw it again for her. She caught on really fast and soon they were having such fun. Whenever Pete threw the ball to a place where Tootsie couldn't see it, she would sniff around until she found it. Pete laughed and laughed as he watched his dog give chase to the ball. She surely had demonstrated that she loved to chase...anything!

Pete recalled one day when Tootsie's chasing got her in trouble with Mom in a big way! The two of them were outside and Pete had the wagon. He was using it to pick up sticks and pine cones from the yard so he could mow. All of a sudden, he heard Mom yelling.

"Pete, Pete! You'd better come get this dog of yours before I do something I'm going to regret!" she called.

Pete went running towards the backyard where she was. As he came around the corner of the house, quite a sight appeared before his eyes. Mom's hens were running around all over the place. They were squawking and clucking; making an awful racket. Feathers were flying all over the place and Mom's face was getting redder and redder as she tried to calm them down. Right in the middle of the chickens was Tootsie having the best game of chase she had ever had. Oh, she thought this was great fun. Mom's hens were free range chickens and that meant they were allowed to roam all over the back yard and in the woods nearby. They came back to the hen house at night to roost and lay their eggs.

"Tootsie, Tootsie! Stop that this minute," called Pete.

"You'd best get that dog out of here before he gets my hens so upset they won't lay eggs," said Mom. "I can't have that because I need all the eggs they will lay for me."

Pete tried to catch Tootsie. Wow! She was fast! She darted away from him and kept right on chasing the hens. "Tootsie, stop that this minute," Pete called. "You come here to me, come on now, here to me! Stop chasing those chickens, this isn't a game play,"

Pete was patting his leg as he called and at the same time trying to inch closer to Tootsie. Finally, he grabbed her and tucked her inside his shirt so she wouldn't wiggle away from again.

After the chickens were settled down and knew they were out of danger from that small enemy, Pete went to see if Mom was okay She had gathered all of the eggs from the nests and was going back into the house.

"Mom, I'm really sorry Tootsie took out after your chickens. We've been having such fun learning to chase things and she didn't know any better. I promise I will teach her to stay away from the hens in the future," Pete apologized.

"I know she hasn't learned that lesson and I will hold you to your promise," said Mom. "She has to learn that there are some things that are off limits around here."

Pete was so glad that Mom wasn't mad at him and he would work hard to teach Tootsie what she could and could not do. He so loved to see her chase and she enjoyed it a lot. But, Pete remembered, there was one time when her chasing after a rabbit had ended with her getting stuck in the rabbit's burrow. It brought a smile to his lips as he thought back on it but when it happened, it hadn't been one bit funny. No siree, it hadn't been the least bit funny at the time.

Chapter Three

Tootsie Goes Underground

It happened one Saturday morning. Pete had finished milking Betsie, the cow, and was carrying the bucket of milk up to the house when he called for Tootsie. She didn't come. "I wonder where that dog is now," he thought. "She and Willow are usually getting in each other's way trying to get into the saucer of warm milk. But only Willow showed up today to enjoy that tasty treat."

"Tootsie," he called again. "Come on girl, it's time to go. Mom is waiting on this milk for breakfast."

Tootsie still didn't come, so Pete went on to the house for breakfast. He said to Mom, "I need to go back down to the barn and see what happened to Tootsie. There's no telling what she may have gotten herself into today. She usually doesn't pass up that warm saucer of milk, but she didn't come when I called."

Back down toward the barn Pete walked. He looked across the yard and along the path carefully but didn't see Tootsie anywhere. It was spring, all the trees were budding and some yellow flowers bloomed along the sides of the yard. The air was fresh and crisp; it was still nippy in the mornings but warmed up by afternoon. He could see lots of little, tender shoots of grass wet from the morning's dew and knew it wouldn't be long before he would need to start mowing the yard again.

As he neared the barn, he called again, "Tootsie, where are you? Come here, girl." Still she didn't come.

His search took him back behind the barn and along the woods. Suddenly, he stopped, thinking he heard a faint something. He stayed very still for a few minutes, just listening to the sounds of the morning. He heard the birds tweeting to one another and watched their horse, Old Bird, shake himself all over after a good roll in the dirt.

There it was again, that sound. His ears pricked up as he heard a soft yipping sound that he thought might be Tootsie. He didn't know where it was. Slowly, he began to inch his way quietly towards the sound. It got louder and louder but he couldn't see Tootsie anywhere. And then he knew what had happened. She had most likely been chasing rabbits again and must have fallen into one of their burrows. Even though they weren't much different in size, the rabbits knew how to move around in their holes and Tootsie didn't. If that is what she did, she would be stuck underground.

Pete walked through the wooded field until he found the entrance to the rabbit hole, well hidden underneath one of the huge rocks. It was likely that Tootsie had spotted a rabbit eating early that morning and had tried to chase it back into its hole. Rabbits like to come out mostly at dawn or evening. Sure enough, Tootsie's yipping sounds were loudest underneath that rock and he could see where the dirt had been disturbed from her digging. He looked the place over and realized he would have to do more digging to get her out. She was stuck tight!

"Well, I reckon you'll stay put until I can get some tools, Tootsie. You sure have gotten yourself in a spot this time," said Pete aloud, as though the dog could hear him. "Those rabbits make a lot of tunnels in their underground burrows with twists and turns so they can have little rooms for all their needs."

He turned around and hurried back to the house.

"Mom, you'll never guess where I found Tootsie!" said Pete. He was almost out of breath from running so hard.

"Where is she? Is she okay?" asked Mom.

"That crazy dog of mine has gone too far this time. She must have chased a rabbit into its hole and then gone in after it. Now, she's stuck and can't turn around to get herself out. I heard her little yips come from under the ground and was

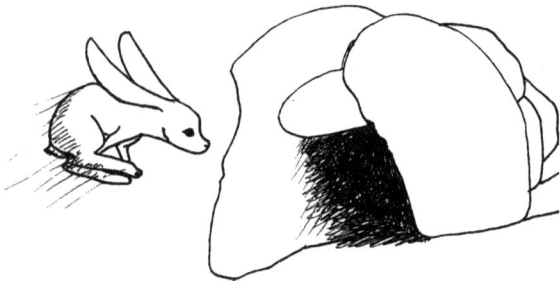

able to follow the sound to find where she is. Now I need a flashlight to help me see how to dig her out. I'll get a shovel from the garden where Dad was working last night but will need to be careful that I don't hit her when I dig!" Pete said.

"Do you think you'll need help?" asked Mom.

"No, if I am careful, I can do it myself. If I have a problem, I'll come and get someone to help," Pete answered as he picked up the flashlight and ran out the back door to the garden for the shovel.

Coming back to the rabbit hole, Pete began to loosen the dirt around the rock at the burrow's entrance. He didn't want to hurt Tootsie but thought that after he was done, the rabbits would not likely use this entrance again. That wasn't really a problem, because they always made several entry ways into their burrows. He could hear her yipping get louder and louder the closer he got to her. He knew she wouldn't have to tunnel in very far to find that she couldn't back herself out of the hole. She didn't have anything on her mind except catching that rabbit, he was sure.

Using his hands as much as he could and the shovel where needed, he dug until he caught sight of a patch of white fur. He tried sticking his arm down into the hole as far as he could reach but he needed a few more inches. His arm just wasn't long enough to reach Tootsie. A little more digging and removing soil and he could touch her and get her into his hands. Shining the flashlight into the hole, Pete could see that the tunnel went down about three feet and then turned a corner to go off in several other directions. Tootsie was caught in that corner. Her body was not able to make the turn like rabbits so that is where she got trapped. Yep, she was really stuck in that hole! After digging some more, Pete reached in as far as his arms would go then pulled and pulled until he finally had her out completely. Was she ever glad to see him! She licked his hands and face and wiggled and wiggled over and over. She was happy to be out of that hole!

"You sure got yourself into a mess that time, didn't you, girl," Pete laughed as he brushed off the dirt and checked Tootsie over to be sure she was okay "Chasing rabbits is a lot of fun, and you just haven't learned that you probably won't catch one unless maybe it is one of those little babies we see hopping all around the yard these spring days. I know you will just keep trying. That's a dog's way and you sure love your little games."

Pete smiled as he remembered the family stories about how his left-handed grandfather could throw a rock so straight and fast that it would hit and kill a rabbit on contact. Rabbit meat was good eating and there had been many times that he had enjoyed rabbit stew. It made him hungry just thinking about it. Eating the rabbits was certainly better than having them eat all their garden stuff. Besides, rabbits had so many babies that there were always plenty to go around.

Carrying Tootsie in his arms, Pete went to return the flashlight and shovel and tell Mom that all was well. Little did he know that day that going down the rabbit hole wasn't the last adventure his little dog would have. She would get herself in many other dangerous situations. Actually, this was just the first of many other rescues.

Chapter Four

The Trap

Another of Tootsie's favorite games was 'hide-and-seek and that one could also get her in trouble. Because of that game, Pete wasn't really surprised when, one Friday afternoon as he got off the school bus, she didn't appear. He thought she was probably hiding somewhere, waiting for his arrival. She always seemed to know the exact time when the bus got to his house so Pete knew she hadn't forgotten him.

"Oh, well, I'll just play along with her", he thought, as he began searching in her favorite hiding places.

He looked under the porch, all through the barn, in the garden, and even looked for her in the places where she liked to dig and hide bones. She was nowhere to be found! After several minutes, he began to get a little worried. This wasn't like Tootsie at all! What if something had happened to her! What if she needed to be rescued again?

"I'll try one more place," he thought. "Sometimes she likes to play and dig over by those big rocks at the edge of the forest."

As Pete neared the forest, he thought he could barely hear whining and the closer he got, the louder the sounds became.

"Tootsie, is that you, girl?" Pete called.

Then Pete heard a yipping bark and knew it was Tootsie. A boy just knows the sound of his own dog's bark.

He began to run toward the forest calling, "Tootsie, where are you? I've been looking all over for you!"

Pete's heart began to beat fast! Surely Tootsie must be hurt or she would have run to meet him. "That has to be why she didn't come to the bus," he thought. He just had to find her and help her.

The barking grew louder. Pete realized that the sounds were coming from inside the forest. All of a sudden, he saw her. She was trapped! It looked like her leg was caught in one of those steel traps like the hunters used. Tootsie was so glad to see Pete that, in spite of her pain, she wagged her tail and licked him all over his face when he bent down to check her leg.

"Ah, girl, what have you done to yourself? Let me look at your leg! Thankfully, that is the only part of you caught in this trap. Otherwise, you would have been done for and I wouldn't like that one bit," said Pete. "If you were chasing rabbits again, you have probably been here in this trap all day! Your foot must have slipped and sprung the trap." He tried to use a calm voice to help comfort Tootsie as he looked at her leg. He knew she must be in a lot of pain because those traps had very sharp points.

"Tootsie, I can't pry this open with only my hands. It's too strong; I'll need some tools. I hate to leave you again but it's the only way. I'll be back soon and have you out of that trap in no time at all. You'll see."

With a final pat to Tootsie's head, Pete turned and ran as fast as his legs would go. He went to the barn where Dad kept his tools and quickly found what he needed. He knew he had to be careful because if his hands slipped, he might cut himself or cause even more harm to Tootsie. He couldn't stand the thought of her being in pain one more minute than was necessary. Again, hurrying as fast as he could, Pete returned to Tootsie.

"Tootsie, I'm coming," he called, "I have the tools and I'll pry you loose as fast as I can."

Placing his tool into the jaws of the trap, Pete pried with all his might. Those traps were tight so it took a lot of effort. Finally he got the jaws opened wide enough to free Tootsie's leg. He carefully removed the lever so that it would not harm either of them.

"Those hunters are going to be mighty disappointed that there is nothing in their trap," he thought, "but I guess it will serve them right. They probably shouldn't even be hunting in this forest anyway."

Holding Tootsie carefully in his arms, Pete took off in a hurry toward the house calling out as he ran, "Mom, Mom! I need you quick! Tootsie's leg is hurt and I need help! Hurry, Mom, hurry!"

Mom heard Pete and came out the door just as Pete entered the yard.

"What's wrong? What happened to Tootsie?" she asked as she wiped her hands on her apron. She had been cooking supper when she heard Pete calling.

"Just look at her, Mom! I found her in the forest with her leg caught in one of those hunter's traps. Just look at her paw! It's cut and bleeding! She must have been there all day," said Pete. He was so worried about Tootsie he could barely think.

Mom took Tootsie from Pete's arms and sat down to look at her. She saw where the trap had made cuts in the dog's leg and carefully checked to see if she was hurt anywhere else.

"Pete", Mom said, "it looks to me like Tootsie's little leg is cut pretty bad. The trap must have caught it in between the points of the trap or else it could have cut off her whole foot. It sure is a good thing she is so small! Since we don't have a veterinarian anywhere around, we'll have to do the best we can to help her heal."

"Tell me what to do, Mom," Pete offered gladly.

"The first thing is to clean it really well. Can you do that while I go look for some medicine and bandages?" asked Mom. "We are going to need to keep this wound clean for several days so that it doesn't get infected."

Pete knew he would do anything to help his little friend. He said, "I'll take her down to the spring and wash her off in that clean water. The coolness will help ease her pain a little. But look at her, Mom, she is such a brave dog that she

41

keeps trying to lick my hand as though I'm the one hurt!" answered Pete.

Soon they were all back at the porch and while Pete held Tootsie tightly, Mom poured some medicine on the cut. Pete knew the medicine would sting and Tootsie might jump away if he didn't hold onto her. "This will help kill any germs she might have gotten from the trap," Mom said, "then we'll bandage the foot so that she can keep it clean while it heals. She won't be able to walk on it for several days."

"I'm glad her bed is right here on the porch," said Pete, "that way I can watch her more carefully. If it's okay with you, Mom, I'd like to sleep out here with her a few nights so I can take good care of her."

"I think that's a good idea, Pete," answered Mom. "You can bring some of your blankets and pillows from your room for yourself. Sweep off the porch first so the bedding won't get dirty; it's still warm enough at night that you won't get too cold. I'm sure Tootsie will feel better with you close by. If she was in the trap all day, she probably hasn't had anything to eat or drink for a good while."

After they made Tootsie comfortable, Pete went to get water for her pan and put it where she could reach it. She really was thirsty and drank so much that Pete had to re-fill the pan before bedtime. He would bring her some food later when he thought she might be ready to eat. He usually fed her with scraps from the table, so he would see what was left tonight after supper. Pete was so glad to have her safe again that he just lay down on the porch and talked with her awhile.

"You need to rest here awhile, Tootsie, so your foot will have time to get well," he said, "it will be hard to get around while it heals. But I'll help you all I can."

After sweeping off the porch, Pete said, "I'll be right back. I'm just going to go get some stuff for my bed. I'll sleep right here beside you all night. You won't have to worry about a thing. I'll take care of everything, you'll see."

That night after supper, Pete fed Tootsie the scraps of left-over food and re-filled the pan of water. After spreading his blankets for the night, he checked her bandaged foot. Most of the bleeding had stopped; that was a good sign. "Sure am glad this is Friday, Tootsie", Pete said, "that way I can watch over you all weekend. If I had to go to school, I might worry about you all day and wouldn't get any schoolwork done!"

As the days went by, Pete took good care of his beloved dog and kept up his regular chores. Her paw was healing nicely and it wasn't long before they were running and playing as usual.

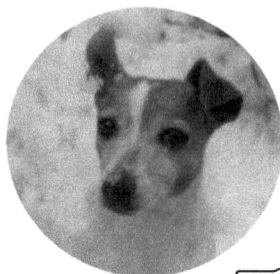

Chapter Five

An Attack at the Spring

Days became weeks and weeks became months, and before he knew it, school was out for the summer. Pete was needed to help with gardens and yard work so his days were filled with activity along with his usual chores. Mom still needed firewood for the cook stove and there was always water to be brought up from the spring. One of Pete's chores was carrying water several hundred yards from the spring to the house. Pete's family didn't have electricity yet so there was no way to pump water uphill and into the house. It would be a few more years before the United Sates Government began a project to provide electricity to the rural areas of the country. In the meantime, Pete carried water. A family surely needed lots of water for drinking, cooking, and washing up. There was always so much work to be done on the farm that Pete was never bored.

One day, when Pete and Tootsie went down to the spring to get water, he heard the dog give

out a yip. He turned just in time to see a snake slithering off into the woods. "Oh, no," Pete cried, "Tootsie, did he get you? Did that snake bite you?"

Dropping the water buckets, Pete quickly

grabbed Tootsie before she could run off after the snake. Knowing her past chasing adventures, she would be likely to do just that. Holding her, he could feel her shaking and quivering from the attempted attack. She was scared. He examined her very closely to see if there were fang marks anywhere. "Looks like you got nipped on the nose, girl. That was a close call; too close to suit me! "Pete said. "I'm going to let Dad look you over and see if that's what he thinks."

Pete carried Tootsie up to the barn where Dad was caring for the cow and horses. "Dad," called Pete, "would you check Tootsie and see if she is okay?"

Dad put down the pitchfork he was using to rake hay down to the animals and said, "Bring her here, son, and let's have a look. Tell me what happened."

"I heard her yelp and saw a snake slithering off into the woods," Pete answered. "I thought it might have bitten her but the only scratches I could find were on her nose. I couldn't see any puncture marks. Dad, if a snake bit her, she'll die, I just know she will!"

"Take it easy, son," said Dad in a calm voice, "let's just be sure there aren't fang marks on her anyplace other than her nose." Dad handled Tootsie gently and looked everywhere for marks. "Pete, I can't find anything that looks like a snake bite. Maybe she jumped out of the way before the snake could get a good hold. Looks like you'll just need to treat the scratches. I think I might have something here in the barn that would do the trick. Did you happen to see what kind of snake it was?" he asked Pete.

"I think it might have been a copperhead, but it happened so fast I'm not sure," Pete answered.

"Well, let's treat this as though it were a poisonous snake," Dad said. He went to the corner where he kept supplies for the animals found some ointment for her scratches.

"Since I can't see any puncture wounds, I am going to assume that she wasn't bitten and that there is no snake venom in her body. But this salve should take care of any infection. It will not stay on her nose too well so you will need to reapply some every few hours," Dad instructed.

He showed Pete just how carefully he must apply the ointment to Tootsie's nose so that it would heal properly. She sure was one lucky little dog to only have scratches from a snake instead of a bite!

"What were you doing when this happened?" asked Dad.

"We were at the spring getting water for the house," Pete replied.

Dad thought a minute then said, "I think I

should go back down there with you and look around to see if I can find that snake. I really don't want to take a chance that a poisonous snake could come anywhere near one of you children or even the animals. If a copperhead were to bite one of the smaller children, it could be deadly! If it really bit Tootsie, she wouldn't make it either because she is so small."

Pete stopped by the house to find his sister. "Martha, would you watch Tootsie for me?" Pete asked. "Dad and I need to go see if we can find that snake. It would be best to keep the other kids inside until we come back. We don't want any of you to be in danger."

He wasn't excited about searching for a dangerous snake but he wasn't as scared with Dad by his side. Life definitely hadn't been the same since Tootsie came into his life. There never seemed to be a dull moment.

Chapter Six

Dad Saves the Day

Pete and Dad were on a mission. They had to make sure the family was as safe as possible from the snakes in the area. They picked up a couple of garden hoes and pulled on their thick rubber boots for extra safety. They didn't want to risk another attack. Then they went searching.

As Pete and Dad walked toward the forest, Dad explained how they would search cautiously for the snake together, but that Pete must let his Dad take charge if they did find it.

"You realize that he may have crawled off into the forest and we would never find him, don't you Pete?" asked his father. "But it would be best to find him and keep him from biting anyone. The forest is one of their favorite places to forage and this is the time of year that the male goes looking for a female so they can have babies. I don't like the thought of a whole nest of copperheads being born so near our home. Sometimes they can have up to 20 babies at one time!"

"How dangerous are copperheads, Dad?" asked Pete. He had heard a lot about them but this was the first time he had seen one for himself. He admitted to himself that this whole thing was a bit scary but he had a lot of trust in his father. Dad would make sure they were okay

"Well," answered Dad, "usually people who are bitten by a copperhead get very sick. Occasionally a person has been known to die from the venom, depending on the size of the person and the region where he lives. In our neck of the woods, the venom is not known to be very deadly and, with proper treatment, a person can survive the bite. But since we are so far away from medical help, it is wise for us to be cautious. Sometimes the copperheads tend to nestle in with the timber rattlers and we don't want to stir up that nest either. Usually, it is best just to leave them alone but when they strike out like they did to Tootsie, I can't let that slide. She must have frightened him and he thought his territory was being invaded."

Pete and Dad were very careful as they searched and searched for the snake all around the spring and out toward the rocks at the edge of the forest. Suddenly Pete saw the snake and immediately stopped. "Hey Dad!" he called, "I think I see it. Come over here and look there on that rock."

Dad quietly and quickly moved over to where Pete was standing and, sure enough, there was the snake sunning himself on a big rock. It was colored tan and brown with large hourglass shaped crossbands down the length of its body.

"It is a copperhead, Pete. You were right," Dad said. "They have sensors that will pick up our heat so we need to be very cautious."

Pete watched as Dad inched his way near the snake then before Pete could believe what

51

had happened, Dad brought the hoe down just on the back of the snake's head cutting it from its body. He then jumped out of the way of the wriggling remains and waited until it was still. He dug a hole and pushed the snake into the hole covering it with dirt. Everything happened so quickly that Pete realized he was shaking all over.

Dad came over to Pete and said, "Are you okay, son?"

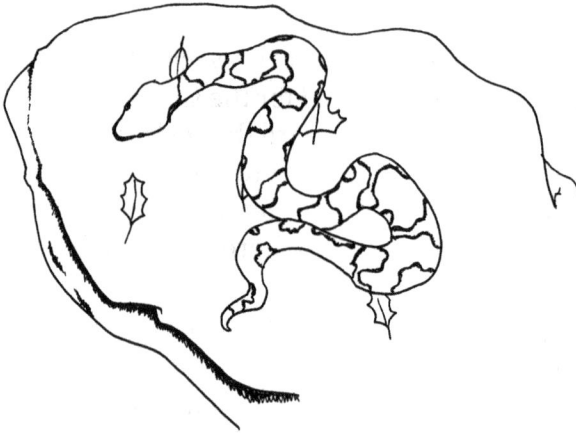

"Yes," said Pete, "but that is an experience I don't want to have to relive ever again. You definitely saved the day and kept us out of danger."

"Well, that isn't something I want you to have to deal with either," said Dad, "although I'm really glad Tootsie was with you when it happened. She probably was the warning you needed so that it wasn't you the snake attacked. It is a blessing that she only got her nose scratched. I'm glad you keep her with you whenever you come this close to the forest. She will alert you to danger and probably even put herself in harm's way before she would let anything happen to you. She is a faithful pet. It was a good day when she came to live with you."

"Hey, Dad," said Pete, "would it be all right with you if we left one of the hoes hanging from a tree branch here at the spring? I think I might feel a bit more safe it we did that."

"That's a fine idea, son," Dad replied, "I think we can spare one just for that purpose. And, to tell the truth, it would make me feel better about things knowing it was there should you have need of it in the future."

When Dad assured himself that Pete was okay, they hung a hoe on a tree branch, then refilled the abandoned water buckets. As they walked home together, Pete thought of the day's adventure and the new dangers to beware of. Living near the forest had always seemed like a good place to live, but he knew that it was wise to know what to watch out for, and how to handle tough situations whenever they happened.

Chapter Seven

Change and Babies

That summer, things began to go badly with Dad's work at the coal mines. Every miner was required to belong to the Union. The 'Union' was a group organized with the idea of protecting the miners' rights. They sat down with the owners of the coal mines and tried to bargain for things like better pay and working conditions for the workers. Any employee who wouldn't agree to belong to the Union wouldn't even be hired in the first place. But, belonging to the Union meant the miners worked when the Union said they could work but had to stay home and not work whenever the Union went on strike. The Union bosses called a strike whenever they couldn't get the coal mine

55

owners to agree to their terms. This meant no work for the miners, and no work meant they got no pay. There had been such good production of coal at the mines recently that the Union wanted more money for the workers but the company didn't agree. So, the Union called a strike which meant Dad couldn't go to work until the disagreement was settled.

No pay meant it would be harder to put food on the table and a family couldn't exist like that for long. Yes, Pete's family had plenty of canned goods that Mom and his sisters had canned from the garden vegetables last summer, but since they had no way of knowing when Dad would get paid again, they had no idea how long that food would have to last. The family had some hard decisions to make.

Pete's older brother John and sister Ora were living in Indiana because there had been no work for them where Pete lived. After a week or so of not knowing when the strike would end, Pete's Mom and Dad decided it was best that Dad go live with Ora where there was work for him in a glass factory. He would send money back home for expenses. If this job went well, it was likely the whole family would move because the doctor had already been telling Dad that his lungs were being damaged by the coal dust in the mines. He had suggested that Dad find other work as soon as possible.

About that time, Pete noticed that Tootsie was pregnant and it looked like she would be having pups in about another month. Pete was excited and worried at the same time. He looked forward to Tootsie's pups but she was so little he just hoped that she would be okay

Weeks passed and Dad's work at the glass factory was going so well that he sent word to Mom to begin preparations to move so they could all be together again. He had found a house that would meet the family's needs and it would be ready for them to move into in about two months. The house was near where Ora lived so Dad thought Mom would be happy there.

Dad said that Mom would need to sell the house, the horses, and the cow. So everybody had jobs to do to get ready to move. There were many boxes to pack and decisions to be made about what to give away or throw away. It was a good thing this news came during the summer because that way Mom would have more help at home. By this time, there was another baby sister named LuAnn in the family and someone would need to watch out for her so Mom could see to all the arrangements.

One morning, several weeks later, Pete stepped out on the porch and saw Tootsie curled up in her bed. Looking closer, he realized that two pups had already been born! Tootsie was struggling to birth a third pup, and Pete could see she was having a hard time because the puppies were too big for her little body. The only thing he knew to do was stay close by, rubbing her head and saying soft words of encouragement to her. He asked Mom to come help her but it was not enough. It was no use. With the birth of that last puppy, Tootsie just gave up. Having babies had been too hard for her, and it took every bit of the life she had just to give birth. When that last puppy was born, she closed her little eyes and breathed her last breath.

When Pete realized she wasn't sleeping from exhaustion, his eyes filled with tears. "Oh, no, Tootsie!" he cried. "You can't leave me. What will I do without you, girl? You're my best friend. I don't want you to be dead!"

Pete picked Tootsie up out of the box, held and hugged her as he rocked back and forth crying. His heart was broken! Nothing would bring his beloved dog back to him. He couldn't imagine life without his precious pet!

Mom just pulled Pete close and said, "Oh, son, I am so sorry!" She put her arms around him, holding him and loving him. There was nothing else she could do but care for her son's hurting heart and cry with him. She knew that

sometimes the best thing you can do when another person hurts is to just hold them and cry with them. After they sat for awhile, Mom knew there were things that needed to be done; they couldn't wait any longer.

"Do you think you could manage to find one of the small, empty moving boxes and put Tootsie there, Pete?" she gently asked.

With tears streaming down his face, Pete went for a box. He also found an old towel that he could use to wrap around her before placing Tootsie in the box. Going back to where Mom waited with the puppies, Pete felt like a big part of his life was missing. His heart was so full of sadness that all he really wanted was to sit on the porch in the quietness and let Mom love on him awhile.

Chapter Eight

Willow to the Rescue

After some time passed, Mom said, "These beautiful little puppies are going to need someone to feed them. They don't know their mother is gone and they will soon be quite hungry. Do you have any idea what we might do?"

"I hadn't even been able to think about that, Mom," said Pete. "Do I need to find a bottle and some milk?"

"Well," said Mom, "I've been thinking and I wonder if Willow would maybe adopt them and feed them. She is nursing her two little kittens but she should have plenty of milk. Sometimes a mother animal will do something like that.

Would you like to try that first?"

"I guess that would be better for them than a bottle. How do we do that?" Pete asked.

"We will just have to bring the puppies to her and see what happens. If she doesn't like the idea then you will have a lot of bottle feeding to do," answered Mom.

Mom began cleaning the birthing fluids off the puppies and freshening the bed. She removed all traces of Tootsie hoping that Willow would be agreeable to nurse the puppies. She really hoped she would go for the idea because if Willow didn't adopt the puppies, it would mean a lot of extra work for Pete. Since Jim had moved away, he was now the oldest one at home so he already had a lot of responsibility. Plus, Pete had also added Dad's chores to his list when Dad went to Indiana and, now all of his extra time was spent helping the family move. With three younger sisters and a brother at home, both Mom and Pete had about all the work they could handle. Mom really depended on Pete these days.

"Well, it just has to work out somehow," Mom sighed as she went in search of Willow. She would bring the puppies to her bed under the porch and just see what would happen. That was the best they could do.

Willow didn't seem to mind when Mom nestled the puppies up to her beside her two kittens. She nuzzled her kittens to be sure they were safe then laid her head back down so they could nurse.

Mom was very gentle when she placed the three new puppies near Willow. She nudged them a bit to encourage them to latch onto Willow's teats. Amazingly, Willow didn't seem to be bothered by the new ones at all! She just lay very still as one by one each little baby puppy latched onto her.

Pete and Mom watched as Willow accepted Tootsie's babies and let them become her family.

"Do you think she will adopt them, Mom?" Pete asked.

"I have known it to happen," replied Mom. "Many kinds of animals have taken over the nursing duties for another animal and adopted them into their own families. We will just watch carefully and see that she doesn't decide to abandon them as they grow. I have an idea that she will treat them just as she does her own babies. It looks to me like she doesn't mind one bit."

"I'll keep an eye on them, especially these first few days," said Pete. "But right now, I have an important job to do. I need to see about Tootsie. I think I need to plan a funeral."

"Do you have an idea where you would like to put her?" asked Mom.

"Yes, I believe I can find someplace for her around here. Let me just have awhile to think about it," said Pete. "I know I will feel better knowing that we took good care of her little body. She seems almost like one of the family and it just wouldn't be right to do it any other way."

"Do you want to tell the other kids, or shall I?" asked Mom.

"Would you do that, please?" Pete asked. "If I have to tell them, I'll probably just stand there and cry and that won't be any help to them. I sure do appreciate all your help, Mom. You let me know that I don't have to do all of this by myself. Thanks for being there for me."

"That's part of being a Mom, son," she said. "I'll just go take care of giving the kids the news right now. They will want to come see the puppies, that's for sure. This way, you can have all the time you need to think about a burial for Tootsie."

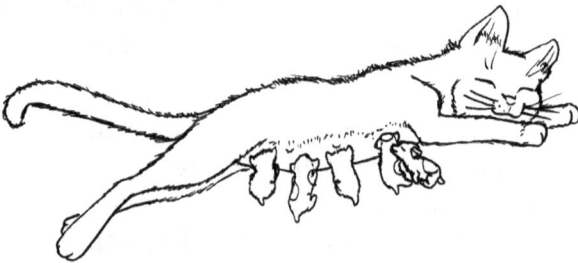

Chapter Nine

The Funeral

Pete put Tootsie and her box down in a safe place on the front porch while he went in search of a site where he could bury her. He walked all around their property, thinking, and finally chose a safe place just behind the barn where the ground was soft. He knew no one would be plowing there and he would fix things so that no animals would be able to reach her. In the barn he found an empty feed sack tossed over in a corner, some string from a bale of hay, and a shovel.

He began to dig the deep grave, all the while trying to hold back the tears in his eyes. "There now," he said aloud when he was finished, "this should be a quiet, undisturbed place for Tootsie."

He walked back to the porch for Tootsie, tucking her wrapped body in the sack. Putting her back into the box, he tied it together with the string then started into the house to tell the family about his plans.

He paused to take another look at Willow nursing Tootsie's three puppies there under the porch. She had cooperated so well! Those puppies looked like having a cat for a mother was the most usual thing in the world! The little puppies' tails were wagging and Willow looked pleased to be their mama. All was well there in that box. Pete sat down on the porch and watched them awhile. Tears began to fill his eyes again knowing that Tootsie's babies would be able to survive. They would be well cared for because Willow was a good mother cat. She would treat them just like they were her very own kittens. She had adopted every one of them. What a wonder!

After awhile, Pete went on into the house to tell his Mom that he was ready to bury Tootsie and asked her if the family wanted to come too. Everybody did. They made a little funeral parade to the back of the barn. Pete was carrying Tootsie in her burial box, Mom carried baby LuAnn, and the sisters Martha and Meg each held one of Wayne's little hands as they came too. When Mom first told them about Tootsie, they had cried; but seeing how well Willow adopted the baby pups made them happy again.

At the burial site, Pete carefully put Tootsie's box into the hole he had dug, and then everyone helped cover it up with dirt. They all shared what they had liked about Tootsie, then Pete asked each person to say one of the Bible verses they learned at church.

Walking back to the house, they sang one of their favorite songs from church, *Jesus Loves Me*. Later, Pete went back to the barn and nailed two pieces of wood together and made a cross to mark the grave. He also found enough rocks to cover the entire area just to be really sure nothing could get to Tootsie.

Pete's heart was very sad for many days after the funeral. My, how he missed Tootsie! They couldn't run and play games together anymore and she would never again greet him at the bus stop after school. There wouldn't be any more rescues, or funny antics to laugh about. She wouldn't be chasing rabbits ever again. He would have to do all his chores by himself with no Tootsie to trot along beside him. He wouldn't be hearing her little yipping voice or see her eyes begging him to play 'fetch'. It felt so lonely. He had grown so used to having her as a part of his life that he didn't know how he would do without her!

Yes, he had a lot of wonderful memories to smile about as he thought of all the ways they had loved each other. She had been the best dog a boy could have, and none other would ever take her place in his heart. He had learned many things from Tootsie, and he knew he had grown up a lot just by taking good care of her. A pet lets a fellow learn about being responsible. Oh, my! She would be missed! Every day, when he thought about her, he would miss her.

Chapter Ten

New Homes for Everyone

Pete enjoyed playing with Tootsie's pups as they grew and before long they were old enough to be weaned from Willow. They could eat food on their own just the same as Willow's kittens. He guessed they would be taking Willow with them when they moved but not the pups.

One day, Mom asked Pete, "Would you like to keep one of these pups and raise it to be your own special dog like Tootsie was?"

"No." said Pete," I have thought about it and I don't think I could ever care for another dog like I did Tootsie. Besides, I know some boys at school who have said they really want one of these pups and they will love them to pieces. They have never had a dog and every boy needs a dog sometime in his life to run and play with, go hunting with, and just love on like the best friend ever. I think it would make me feel really good to see those boys happy with a dog of their own. Besides, didn't you say that the new place Dad found was near the town?"

"Yes, that is what we've heard," said Mom.

"Well then I don't think I would want to have a dog that couldn't run and play with me. There won't be woods and fields there," Pete said. "No, I think that Tootsie's memories and adventures will have to be enough for me."

"I just wanted you to know that if you did want one, we would try and work something out, no matter what it is like wherever we live," Mom assured Pete.

"Thanks, Mom," answered Pete.

One by one the friends from school began coming for Tootsie's pups, all of which would grow to be bigger than Tootsie ever was. Each little pup had a lot of white fur just like Tootsie, but there were some brown spots here and there that could have come from her or their father. Pete never figured out what dog was the father of Tootsie's babies. He just knew that he had to have been much bigger than Tootsie or she wouldn't have had trouble giving birth.

Pete enjoyed watching as the boys made

their selections and began getting acquainted together. It was great fun seeing their happy faces as they held their new pet and talked about names. Pete hadn't given the puppies names because he wanted the boys to have that joy for themselves. The little puppies wagged their tails and licked the boys' faces. It made Pete remember how Tootsie had done the same thing to him when she first came to be his dog. These boys were sure to have some happy days ahead. It seemed to be another case of love at first sight!

Watching each of the boys come and claim their pup, Pete saw that they were so full of joy that he knew he had done the right thing. All the pups would have new homes and the boys would have lots of adventures and challenges ahead as they learned to take care of the pups and watch them grow.

Very soon now, his family would move to their new home as well. Pete thought that it had turned out to be a good time to move. Staying here would only make him think more and more about what he had lost because it seemed like everywhere he looked, he saw something that reminded him of Tootsie. Moving to a new place would give him something new to think about. Besides, he would be finishing high school next year, and he had plans to make for the rest of his life. It had been good living here in Kentucky, but he began to wonder what it would be like in Indiana.

On moving day, Pete's sister Ora sent some of her friends with a big truck to take all their things to Indiana. Pete had loved living here with his grandfather nearby. He would miss his friends, the forests and the wide open fields that had been so much a part of his childhood days. He had grown up here and it would always have a special place in his heart no matter where he lived.

Pete never again had a dog of his own but he learned not to be sad about that. He knew no other dog could replace Tootsie in his heart. From time to time, his family would see him just sitting and thinking. If they could have looked into his mind and read his thoughts, they wouldn't have been surprised to find that he was thinking back on those wonderful days when he roamed the hillsides and forests with Tootsie.

www.ingramcontent.com/pod-product-compliance
Lightning Source LLC
Chambersburg PA
CBHW060144050426
42448CB00010B/2296

The Seven Great Monarchies of The Ancient Eastern World by George Rawlinson

Volume III (of VII) The Third Monarchy: Media

George Rawlinson was born on 23rd November 1812 at Chadlington, Oxfordshire. He was the younger brother to the eminent Assyriologist, Sir Henry Rawlinson.

Rawlinson took his degree at Trinity College, Oxford in 1838. Here he also enjoyed playing cricket and was considered to have been a rare talent at the sport. In 1840 he was elected to a fellowship at Exeter College, Oxford. After being ordained in 1841 he became, from 1842 to 1846, a tutor there as well.

In 1846 Rawlinson married Louisa, the daughter of Sir RA Chermside.

His progress continued to be rapid and varied in acknowledgement of his undoubted talents. In 1859 he was made a Bampton lecturer, and was Camden Professor of Ancient History from 1861 to 1889.

By 1872 Rawlinson was appointed canon of Canterbury, and after 1888 he was rector of All Hallows, Lombard Street.

In 1873, he was made proctor in Convocation for the Chapter of Canterbury.

As a scholar he produced, either on his own or in collaboration, several works which are greatly thought of even to this day. His translation of the History of Herodotus (in collaboration with Sir Henry Rawlinson and Sir John Gardiner Wilkinson), 1858–60; The Five Great Monarchies of the Ancient Eastern World, 1862–67; which was later expanded to include The Sixth Great Oriental Monarchy (Parthian), 1873; and The Seventh Great Oriental Monarchy (Sassanian), 1875. Among his other works were Manual of Ancient History, 1869; Historical Illustrations of the Old Testament, 1871; The Origin of Nations, 1877; History of Ancient Egypt, 1881; Egypt and Babylon, 1885; History of Phoenicia, 1889; Parthia, 1893; Memoir of Major-General Sir HC Rawlinson, 1898.

His lectures to an audience at Oxford University on the topic of the accuracy of the Bible in 1859 were published as the apologetic work The Historical Evidences of the Truth of the Scripture Records Stated Anew in later years.

Despite this somewhat prodigious output and alongside his other clerical and family duties he contributed to the Speaker's Commentary, the Pulpit Commentary, Smith's Dictionary of the Bible, and various similar publications.

George Rawlinson died on 7th October, 1902 in Canterbury.

Index of Contents

Index of Illustrations

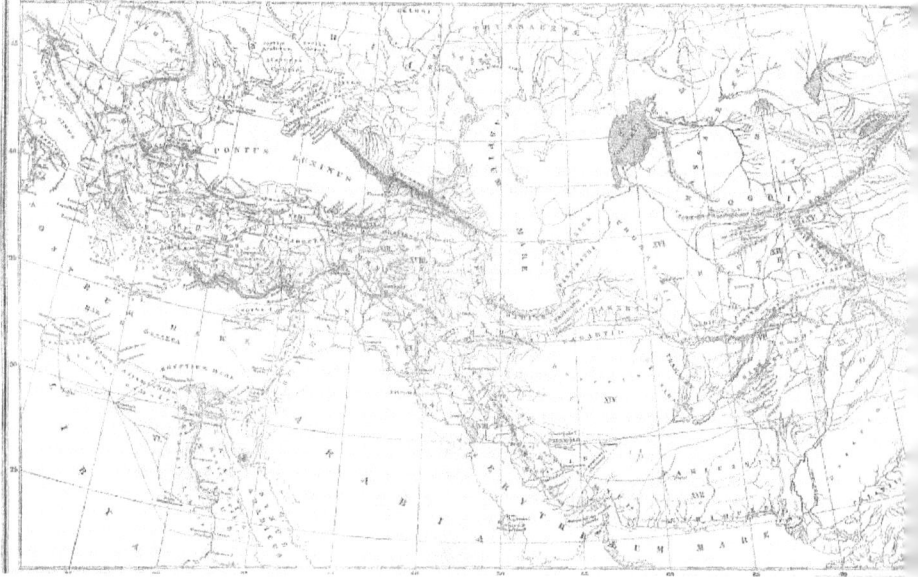

CHAPTER I

DESCRIPTION OF THE COUNTRY

Along the eastern flank of the great Mesopotamian lowland, curving round it on the north, and stretching beyond it to the south and the south-east, lies a vast elevated region, or highland, no portion of which appears to be less than 3000 feet above the sea-level. This region may be divided, broadly, into two tracts, one consisting of lofty mountainous ridges, which form its outskirts on the north and on the west; the other, in the main a high flat table-land, extending from the foot of the mountain chains, southward to the Indian Ocean, and eastward to the country of the Afghans. The western mountain-country consists, as has been already observed, of six or seven parallel ridges, having a direction nearly from the north-west to the south-east, enclosing between them, valleys of great fertility, and well watered by a large number of plentiful and refreshing streams. This district was known to the ancients as Zagros, while in modern geography it bears the names of Kurdistan and Luristan. It has always been inhabited by a multitude of warlike tribes, and has rarely formed for any long period a portion of any settled monarchy. Full of torrents, of deep ravines, or rocky summits, abrupt and almost inaccessible; containing but few passes, and those narrow and easily defensible; secure, moreover, owing to the rigor of its climate, from hostile invasion during more than half the year; it has defied all attempts to effect its